Dad's War

STORIES AND REMEMBRANCES

June 1944 to October 1945

Leslie J. Ungers

Copyright © 2016 by Leslie J. Ungers

All rights reserved.

No part of this publication may be reproduced, stored in a retrieval system, or transmitted, in any form or by any means, electronic, mechanical, photocopying, recording, or otherwise, without prior permission.

Cover illustration: Courtesy of www.theshermantank.com
Cover design by L. J. Ungers
Photographs: Army Archive/National Archives

In memory of Dad

Wars may be fought with weapons, but they are won by men.
— GENERAL GEORGE S. PATTON, JR.

Preface

This is an account of the stories told to me by my father Ralph Joseph Ungers, former Technical Sergeant, Third Grade variously assigned to the Headquarters, A, and D Companies of the 749th Tank Battalion.

These stories cover Dad's experiences at Fort Knox during stateside training and while in combat during the war in Europe. A few of these stories, told to me as a boy, were either humorous or ones that Dad felt taught a lesson. As far as can I remember, they were neither planned nor told to me in any particular order; they were just remembrances Dad would share as they occurred to him. Later in life, particularly after Dad suffered a minor stroke in his fifties, he started to talk to me about the nature of war and the extent of his involvement. It was at this point that the stories started to assume a chronological order, and he began to associate some of them with specific military units, events, and places. This is also when Dad started to share some of his darker experiences—ones he would not have told a young boy. By my adulthood, I was also learning from Dad more of the technical aspects of armored vehicles and the details of army life in a combat zone.

I am writing this now after encouragement from friends, with whom I have shared a few of the stories, and from my wife, Priscilla, who correctly points out that since Dad's experiences were not shared with other family members, their telling is my responsibility or else they will be lost with me.

In addition to Dad's remembrances, I have, over the years, acquired photographs and other pieces of information regarding his unit, the battles he fought in, and the nature of the armored forces he served with. These are added as appropriate to help the reader understand Dad's situation, his progress across Europe, and his advancement from private to non-commissioned officer.

I have tried to confirm as much of what Dad told me from other sources. Undoubtedly, his retelling of stories and the passage of time have clouded some of the details and overstated others. However, where comparisons could be made, it is remarkable how well Dad's remembrances agree with the information in published records, unit histories, and other accounts of his tank battalion.

To my siblings, Lori and Jayne; Dad's grandchildren and great grandchildren; and their children; I hope you find reading these stories as enjoyable and rewarding as I did listening to Dad tell them.

Proud son of a Tanker,
Leslie Joseph Ungers
August 2016

Table of Contents

Preface   vii

Enlistment and the Draft   3

Basic Training   5

The North Atlantic   8

France   11

Lorraine   18

Ardennes   22

Rhineland   26

Crossing the Rhine   33

Central Europe   36

Casualty of War   39

Homecoming   43

Future Past   47

Who Dad Was   49

Army Formations   52

Bibliography   53

Illustrations and Photographs

Dad at Fort Knox	5
Mortar carrier bogged down near Nancy, France	12
Dad and his Sherman tank	15
Dad's travel to the front and movements during combat	17
German Tiger next to a Sherman tank	20
American troops passing through the Siegfried Line	26
Stuart light tank	28
Chaffee light tank	29
Landkern, Germany	31
German 88 mm anti-tank gun	39
AeroMed L5 single-engine aircraft	41
Hospitel Hôtel-Dieu de Paris	42
Bill Edwards and Dad	45
Dad's decorations	46
Sergeant Ungers and a Sherman	48

Dad's War

STORIES AND REMEMBRANCES

June 1944 to October 1945

Leslie J. Ungers

Dad's War

Dad's War

Enlistment and the Draft

Ralph Joseph Ungers was known to his parents as "Ralph," to his friends as "Joe," but to me as "Dad." Born into a working class family with aspirations, his father, Henry, would eventually acquire a farm, store, and plumbing business, before losing the store and business during the Great Depression. Being a child at the time, Dad would only remember the farm. He would come to love rural living but lament his station in life as a "poor farmer." The Depression would be one of two experiences that would shape Dad's personality—the other would be World War II.

As a grandson of German immigrants, Dad remembered paying attention to the situation in Europe in the early 1940s, but like most Americans, he showed little interest in Japan's aggression on the Asian mainland. His grandfather, Mathias, and his father, Henry, were also concerned about Europe, but Mathias had purposely left Germany in the late 1800s, and Henry spent an unpleasant tour of duty at sea during World War I. Although proud to be German-Americans, neither wanted anything to do with the "Old World." As for Asia, it was just too far away to cause concern. All that changed when, in December, during Dad's sophomore year of high school, news broke that Japan had bombed Pearl Harbor.

Dad wanted to enlist in the navy and fight the Japanese; he wanted to be a sailor just as his father had been. Henry had enlisted at seventeen and served on four ships: starting as a trainee on the USS *Constellation*, the last sailing frigate of the US Navy that is now a floating museum in Baltimore's Inner Harbor; then as a Seaman on the USS *Missouri*, a battleship of Teddy Roosevelt's "Great White Fleet"; then on the USS

Wyoming, a prewar dreadnought; and finally, ending his career as a Petty Officer on the SS *El Oriente*, a transport ship during World War I.

Dad never mentioned what his father thought of him trying to enlist, but his mother, Lena, refused to hear of it. Dad would have to wait until his eighteenth birthday, and then it would be without his mother's blessing. In September 1943 Dad turned eighteen; however, the big event was delayed again, when he injured his leg playing football and couldn't stand for the enlistment physical. On finishing his senior year, and while waiting on graduation, Dad again considered an attempt at the navy. However, before he could act, or his mother could protest, a telegram arrived directing him to report to an army enlistment center. Dad told this story often and usually ended it with a bootcamp song of the era:

> *You're in the army now,*
> *you're not behind the plow;*
> *you'll never get rich,*
> *you son-of-a-bitch,*
> *you're in the army now!*

The irony was not lost on Dad; he had wanted to enlist in the navy and fight the Japanese, but fate would have him drafted into the army to fight the Germans of his heritage

---

Dad Defends the Bedroom

Grandpa Henry used to tell how he and Grandma were awakened in the night by a voice in their bedroom. "Japs," the voice declared. "The Japs are coming!" Henry turned on the light to find his first-born son armed with a broomstick and in the midst of sleepwalking. Henry said Dad was determined to get under the bed and it took several minutes to convince him it wasn't necessary, the Japanese weren't in Ohio, and he could go back to his own room.

Basic Training

As a new recruit in the army, Dad was assigned to basic training or "bootcamp" at the Armored Force Replacement Training Center in Fort Knox, Kentucky in June of 1944.[1]

Dad at Fort Knox
Summer 1944

Dad, along with hundreds of other new recruits, boarded trains bound for their respective bootcamps. As chance would have it, Dad's trip would be delayed while making connections at Union Terminal in Cincinnati, Ohio. With a few hours to kill, Dad and a number of other recruits decided to take cabs to Northern Kentucky to visit a few of the bars and nightclubs before heading on to Louisville.[2] The excursion lasted longer than expected and the group missed their connecting

---

[1] Date of enlistment was 10 June 1944. As accessed on May 21, 2016 at https//aad.archives.gov.

[2] Before the growth of Las Vegas, Northern Kentucky was famous for its gambling and nightclubs. Following the repeal of Prohibition, and then well into the 1960s, these nightclubs played host to celebrities like Frank Sinatra, Bing Crosby, and Bob Hope. Ref.: Linduff, J. et al. *When Vice Was King - a History of Northern Kentucky Gambling, 1920–1970*, as accessed on July 17, 2016 at http://www.preservinggaminghistory.com.

train. Dad commented that the little adventure proved to be a very bad idea. He didn't elaborate other than to say that the army did not appreciate having a number of its new recruits "AWOL" from their first day in the service.[3]

    Fort Knox is located approximately twenty-five miles southwest of Louisville, Kentucky. It was the camp where recruits bound for duty in the armored forces[4] would receive seventeen weeks of training before being assigned to an army unit. The training involved standard bootcamp indoctrination and physical fitness, as well as instructions in hand-to-hand combat, small arms, mortars, tank guns, vehicle operation and maintenance, chemical warfare, and other subjects necessary to prepare replacements for the armored forces.[5] Dad would eventually be rated as an Expert—the army's highest qualification—in the rifle, carbine, machine gun, sub-machine gun, and tank weapons, and as a Sharpshooter—the army's second highest rating—in the 81 mm mortar.

    He didn't talk much about basic training, other than saying that, unlike portrayals by Hollywood, his drill instructor was an old cavalry sergeant who Dad claimed, "…was as kind and sweet a man as any grandfather." According to Dad, he seldom yelled, took a real interest in his men, and treated them more like sons than recruits. All that said, Dad noted that having a great guy as a drill instructor didn't save his squad from being introduced to army hazing, and like all recruits who did their

---

[3] AWOL is an acronym for "absent without leave."

[4] Created in 1940, the Armored Force took control of all tank units previously assigned to infantry and cavalry units during World War I.

[5] As accessed on May 15, 2016 at https://www.knox.army.mil/about/history.aspx.

basic training at Fort Knox, Dad remembered his introduction to the training hills, named Misery, Agony, and Heartbreak.

> **Tanks Not Planes**
>
> Dad would tell me the story how—now that he was stuck in the Army—he tried to get into flight school. In 1944 the air force was not yet a separate service; it was part of the army and known as the "Army Air Corp." While Dad stood in line at the recruitment center, a sergeant walked up and asked how many recruits wanted to get out of the infantry. Thinking this was his chance to talk his way into flight school, Dad raised his hand. The sergeant pulled Dad out of the line, and before Dad could speak, he barked, "Congratulations son, you're going to Armor School!"

The North Atlantic

In October 1944 Technician, Fifth Grade (T/5) Ralph Joseph Ungers left Fort Knox on a train bound for the East Coast, along with scores of other newly minted GIs.[6] As a T/5, Dad had achieved the rank of corporal upon completing his training. In the 1940s army, a T/5 was the rank and pay grade of a corporal, but with special training in specific weapons or vehicles. Technical specialists would deal with the issues of operating vehicles, weapon systems, or other mechanical equipment, and only took on leadership roles when another person of rank was incapacitated. Sadly, this was to be a common experience for Dad during the war. On several occasions, he had to assume leadership of his tank or squad upon the injury or death of its commander.

T/5 Insignia

Arriving in New York City early, Dad had several hours to kill before reporting for duty and boarding a troopship bound for England. Dad narrated how he was in a bar in Manhattan and ran into a couple of sailors, who just happened to be from the same ship he was assigned to for the crossing. Wondering what a transit of the North Atlantic would be like, Dad befriended the sailors, bought a round of beers, and plied them with questions. In gratitude for the beer, Dad was told what to expect and given advice on how to "game" the system onboard ship. The sailors told

---

[6] GI, was slang for any American service man—in the army, navy, or marines. It was taken from army stamps on equipment that were made of galvanized iron. Later, the initialism was associated with the stamp "Government Issue," common on papers, boxes, or records of the time.

him that army troops could signup to stand night watch while at sea. Although one might think this a lousy job, the sailors informed Dad that staying up all night watching for enemy submarines was, in fact, a "cushy job." Soldiers who participated in the night watch had no other assigned duties during the day, would sleep in navy bunks with a mattress and clean sheets, eat hot chow, and would be allowed to walk the deck in the fresh air any time they wanted. This is in contrast to the other army troops onboard ship, who had to stay below decks, sleep on canvas cots, train during the day, and were only allowed topside for a few hours during rotations. Dad said the first thing he did when he got onboard was to locate a petty officer and volunteer for watch duty.

> **High Seas**
>
> Dad recalls at least one day of rough seas during the crossing, and he remembers having to eat several of his meals while standing. The ship would roll so much to port and then to starboard that the dishes would not stay put on top of the mess tables. Cups and saucers slid all over, and it was hard to keep the coffee in your mug. He recounted that, during one meal, the sea was so bad, and the ship listed (tilted) so much that he had to stand with one foot on the deck of the mess hall and the other on the wall (bulkhead), just to keep the food on his plate!

Dad never saw a U-boat[7] during the crossing, but he did observe several flashes on the horizon. He was told these were Allied ships in

---

[7] A German submarine, abbreviation of *Unterseeboot* or "undersea boat".

their convoy[8] that had been hit by torpedoes and sunk. After that, Dad admitted, he found it hard to sleep, worrying that his ship might be next. He remembers that almost everyone onboard the troopship slept fully dressed with their life preservers on and their boots nearby.

---

[8] A group of ships traveling together for mutual support and protection. During World War II, convoys crossing the North Atlantic consisted of supply and troopships that were protected by combat vessels like battleships, cruisers, and destroyers. Convoys could number between thirty and seventy ships.

France

Dad landed in England and was immediately shipped across the English Channel to Normandy, France, where he was loaded on a transport truck along with other replacements. Dad entered the war in the late fall of 1944—well after the June 6, D-Day Invasion of Normandy, and just at the end of General George S. Patton, Jr.'s historic advance across France. Upon arriving in Europe, Dad was assigned to the 749th Tank Battalion, which was attached to Patton's Third Army, then fighting in the vicinity of Nancy, France.

The 749th was a "independent tank battalion," which referred to a battalion that was not a permanent part of any particular armor or infantry formation, but would be attached to other units as needed.[9] Typically, the these tank battalions accompanied infantry units into battle, and provided direct or indirect fire support.[10] Other times, the independent tank battalions would be added to the

Shoulder patch

---

[9] Army tank battalions consisted of six companies: a battalion headquarters, a service company, and four tank companies (designated A, B, C, and D). Each tank company consisted of four units: a company headquarters and three tank platoons. Each tank platoon consisted of five tanks.

[10] Direct fire was when a tank attacked a line-of-sight target. It involved the act of locating the target, aiming and firing. Indirect fire involved the use of spotters or forward observers, who would call or radio back to the tank to "lob" shells on a target that the tank's gunner could not see. The indirect process involved estimating the direction, the distance to the target, and the angle of fire, then making corrections to each until the target was hit.

strength of a larger Combat Command formation[11] that was organized in anticipation of a specific mission. Independent tank battalions were also employed as defensive forces to repel enemy counterattacks. Although the 749th would perform all these duties, Dad remembers most often supporting advancing infantry troops.

Mortar carrier bogged down near Nancy, France
Fall 1944
(Dad is the soldier pointing to the vehicle)

Dad's first job as a combat soldier was that of a weapons specialist on an armored mortar[12] carrier. These carriers were organized under

---

[11] A combat command is a formation that did not have dedicated battalions. Instead, tank, armored infantry, and armored field artillery battalions, as well as smaller units of engineers and cavalry were grouped together under a single command.

[12] A mortar is a weapon that fires projectiles at low velocities and short distances. The mortar has traditionally been used as a weapon to propel explosive shells in high-arcing trajectories.

the battalion's headquarters (HQ) as part of a mortar platoon. The vehicle was a mobile platform for an 81 mm mortar that was used against enemy infantry, machine gun emplacements, or lightly armored vehicles. While in combat, the carrier crew would deploy to a location just behind the front line and then respond to requests for indirect fire from a forward observer. Depending on the type of shell used, the mortar had a range of approximately two hundred to two thousand yards. Dad admitted being proud of their performance as a mortar crew. His team had a reputation for being able to hit the target on the second or third round almost every time.

Dad never mentioned how long he was with Battalion HQ, but his next assignment came soon, and it was as a tank driver for the battalion combat tank companies A and D.[13] Dad was with A Company during the first few campaigns before being transferred to D Company, which would be Dad's home for most of his time in Europe. There he made several friends, many of whose names he could recall even late in life.

The five-man, medium-weight Sherman tank served as the army's main tank throughout the war. When it was first introduced in North Africa in 1943, the Sherman was as good as most German armor in the field; however, by late 1944 it had been surpassed by larger and more advanced German models. Although the Sherman could still put up a good fight against the medium-sized German Panther tank (introduced in 1943), it was hopelessly out-armored and out-gunned by the heavier Tiger tank (introduced in 1941). Despite these weaknesses, Dad felt the

---

[13] At the start of the war, the typical tank battalion was composed of six companies: a headquarters company, a service company, three medium tank companies (A, B, and C), and a light tank company (D). Near the end of the war, the light tank companies were being converted to medium tank companies.

Sherman had several advantages: it was more reliable than either the Panther or Tiger; it was comparatively fast; it had a quicker turning turret that greatly improved its rate of fire; and finally, it had a gyroscopic mounted gun site that allowed it to "aim on the run"—as opposed to the German tanks that had to stop to reliably aim before firing. When properly deployed, as in the support of infantry, he thought it a very good weapon of war.[14]

Dad's first tank was an early version of the Sherman, designated an M4. His vehicle had seen earlier service in North Africa, but had been refitted and armored-up for use in Europe. Like all M4 Sherman tanks, it was equipped with a 75 mm main gun, a 30-caliber coaxial machine gun[15], a 30-caliber bow machine gun, and a 50-caliber machine gun on the turret. The M4 was powered by a nine-cylinder, air-cooled radial aircraft engine built by the Wright Aeronautical.[16] Dad liked it, because it was very easy to service, and being air-cooled, "…you never needed to worry about the radiator freezing." It was, however, so loud, Dad said, "the Germans could hear you coming for miles."

As was the practice, tank crews named their tanks, just as pilots named their aircraft, and Dad's first tank carried the hopeful moniker, *"We'll Make It."*

---

[14] After World War II, the Sherman tank saw combat in the Korean War, the Arab-Israel Wars, and other conflicts, well into the 1960s. As accessed on May 10, 2016 at http://en.wikipedia.org/wiki/M4_Sherman.

[15] Located next to the tanks main gun, the coaxial machine gun was used against infantry and other "soft" targets when use of the main gun would be excessive.

[16] Wright Aeronautical, founded by the pioneering Wright brothers, was a manufacturer that built aircraft and was a supplier of aircraft engines to other builders. In 1929 it merged with Curtiss to form Curtiss-Wright. As accessed on May 10, 2016 at http://en.wikipedia.org/wiki/M4_Sherman.

Dad and his Sherman tank
Winter 1944

The New Guy

Dad described how every replacement had to earn the confidence of his squad. No one wanted to go into battle with a completely "green" recruit. In particular, veteran tankers didn't want a new crew member to hesitate or get sick when confronted with the blood and gore of combat. It was believed that the sooner a person confronted some of the realities of war, the sooner he would become a reliable comrade-in-arms. In Dad's unit, replacements like him were acclimated by having them check the bodies of the dead. The task was ordered under the pretense of a need to make sure the enemies were in fact dead and not faking. In truth, Dad said, the bodies selected for inspection were those that had been in the field decaying for several days. It was a very unpleasant experience; but because Dad had been raised on a farm, where he helped with the slaughtering of animals for market, he said he handled it pretty well. Dad felt bad for the guys who had never lived or worked on a farm. In addition to getting sick, they were horrified by the experience. However, Dad didn't escape completely unaffected. While he was removing the helmet of one dead German soldier, Dad once told me, "the top of his head came off in my hands; I lost my lunch on the spot."

Dad's War

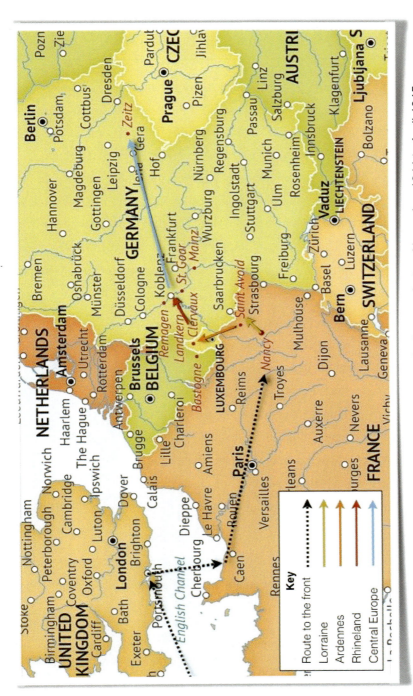

Dad's travels to the front and movements during combat — November 1944 to April 1945

Lorraine

South of Luxembourg, Patton's Third Army fought from September until mid-December to push the Germans out of the Lorraine region of France. Crossing the Moselle River and capturing fortifications in the area proved difficult for the American troops in the face of German reinforcements, American supply shortages, and unfavorable weather. In November, however, the German front broke under repeated Allied attacks, resulting in advances that placed the Third US Army on the western frontier of Germany. The entire campaign in Lorraine lasted from September 1944 through January 1945, but Dad's involvement occurred in November and December 1944.

Although Dad was not specific about exactly when it took place, at some point, while fighting in Lorraine, he received a promotion to Sergeant, Technician Fourth Grade (T/4). Dad said that his advancement from corporal to sergeant involved more responsibilities and a pay raise. He also noted that it was not a very good deal, for although there was plenty of work: "…there was no time nor place to spend the money."[17]

T/4 Insignia

During this time, Dad remembered that most of his combat activity involved guarding key bridges and providing long hours of indirect fire support for infantry fending off German counterattacks.

---

[17] In 1944, a corporal made approximately $2 a day, while a sergeant made the princely sum of $2.58 a day. Ref.: *Barron's National Business and Financial Weekly*, 24 April 1944.

Battle Eggs

In Dad's opinion, the best army rations were the canned cheese and powdered eggs. But Dad and his crew liked the powdered eggs most and would trade other rations for extra tins. "We even built our own grill," he said. When his tank was providing indirect fire support, a lot of the time was spent just loading and firing the 75 mm main gun. The cannon would get so hot, "You could fry an egg on it, so we decided to do just that." A grill was made by welding a piece of armor plate to the top of the breach. As the gun heated up, the weld would transfer the heat to the metal plate. When the firing stopped, Dad said, "You had a nice, hot grill, and with a little oleo (margarine), we would scramble our eggs."

It was in Lorraine that Dad had his first encounter with a German Tiger tank. His company was in the process of supporting infantry in the countryside near the German border, when reports came of a Tiger tank advancing on the battalion's position. Dad's platoon was tasked with locating and dealing with the Tiger.

Throughout the war, the Tiger tank was universally feared by American tankers, because no single Sherman tank could go toe-to-toe with this German heavy tank; and indeed, a whole platoon of M4 Sherman tanks could be decimated by a single Tiger.

Seven inches of armor protected the Tiger, whereas four inches of forward armor protected Dad's M4 Sherman.[18] The Sherman's medium velocity 75 mm main gun could not penetrate the Tiger's forward armor, even at distances under a hundred yards—this in comparison with

---

[18] As accessed on May 10, 2016 at https://en.wikipedia.org/wiki/Tiger_II.

the Tiger tank that was equipped with a high velocity 88 mm main gun that could penetrate the Sherman's forward armor at distances of well over a mile![19]

German Tiger next to a Sherman tank
Winter 1944

Understandably, once the lead elements of his platoon located the Tiger, Dad said the platoon leader called in an air strike. Soon a pair of Republic P-47 Thunderbolt fighter aircraft showed up and hit the Tiger with volleys of high velocity wing rockets.[20] Dad said the otherwise for-

---

[19] Penetration figures using American and British success criteria allowing direct comparison to foreign gun performance. Ref.: Livingston, R., et al. *WWII Ballistics: Armor and Gunnery*.

[20] The Republic P-47 Thunderbolt was a World War II era aircraft produced by the United States between 1941 and 1945. Its primary armament was eight 50-caliber machine guns, four per wing, but in the fighter-bomber ground-attack role it could carry rockets or a bomb load of 2,500 pounds. As accessed on May 11, 2016 at https://en.wikipedia.org/Republic_P-47_Thunderbolt.

midable Tiger "…didn't stand a snowball's chance in hell." After that, Dad remembered "How wonderful it was to hear the sound of P47s flying overhead!"

The 749th Tank Battalion participated in defensive operations in Lorraine throughout the early part of December, while one of the most historic events of the war was about to take place just to the north of the Third US Army's position.

Ardennes

The great counteroffensive of the war in Western Europe was known to the Germans as operation "Watch on the Rhine" and to the Allies as the "Ardenne Counteroffensive." However, the press would dub this historic clash of arms as the "Battle of the Bulge." It was so named because of the characteristic bulge the German attack created in the Allied lines. Intending to divide the Allied armies and capture the key seaport of Antwerp, Belgium, the German army secretly amassed and hid over 450,000 troops and 1,200 armored vehicles along its western border and readied them for an attack through the Ardennes Forest of southern Belgium.

The Allies believed the Ardennes to be too mountainous and forested for use as a winter route of attack. They considered it a "quiet front," useful for training replacements and resting over worked troops. Taking advantage of the bad weather that kept the Allied air forces grounded, the Germans penetrated the Allies' front line in this lightly defended sector. When the attack occurred on 16 December 1944, the German successes came quick and resulted in a deep, fifty-mile penetration of the American lines before the Allies were able to regroup. It was a bold and unexpected move that caught the First US Army completely by surprise, sending it into an unorganized retreat.

In a move that would be the crowning achievement of Patton's career, on December, 26 1944, the Third US Army would pivot, turn north, and throw three fully equipped divisions into the fight in less than forty-eight hours. Penetrating the southern shoulder of the Bulge, Patton's action disrupted the German attack and gave other Allied units time to organize a defense. In addition to helping stop the German advance, Patton's maneuver relieved the 101st Airborne Division that had been surrounded at the Belgian village of Bastogne. Although ultimately a massive German defeat, the Battle of the Bulge would cost the American Army 89,000 troops—killed, wounded, or missing-in-action—more casualties than any other battle in American history.

Dad's company joined the Ardennes fight as part of the more easterly elements that entered Luxembourg, while the main body of Patton's Third Army raced toward Bastogne. Leaving defensive positions near Saint-Avold, France, Dad's company crossed into Luxembourg and moved toward the German frontier in the area just north of the Moselle River.[21]

During the war, Western Europe was experiencing the coldest winter on record. Temperatures in Luxembourg dropped to below freezing during December 1944 and January 1945. This was a problem for all Allied soldiers and tankers were no exception. During the day, when the tank was running, it provided shelter and escape from the cold. But when the tank was not running, the crew compartment became a "frozen coffin," because the tank was not insulated. When in bivouac at night, you had a choice to stay in the tank, or find a snowdrift, burrow in, and, "like the Eskimos," create an igloo-like shelter. Dad said, the snow was an amazingly good insulator, you'd wake up in the morning cold and wet, but alive. A person could sleep through almost anything, when phys-

---

[21] It was at this point Dad remembers having lost physical contact with the rest of the battalion. The after action reports for the 749th Battalion, which were very detailed for events prior to the Battle of the Bulge, now became confused and placed several platoons of the D Company with different units. Consistent with Dad's memory, elements of D Company were no longer being properly accounted for by the battalion reports.

ically and mentally exhausted after a day of battle. Dad said that several times, tankers who chose to sleep in the tank's crew compartment simply fell asleep and froze to death.

> **Five Steaks per Cow**
>
> The American soldier, if nothing else, was resourceful. Dad recounted coming across a stray cow that had escaped from its barn as a result of the fighting. Having survived on nothing more than water and K-rations for several days, the crew of *We'll Make It* saw the cow as a delicious opportunity. One well-placed round from an M1 carbine yielded five fresh beef steaks. Dad said that this type of foraging was against orders, and having been raised on a farm, he admitted having regrets about the wastefulness of taking only five steaks and leaving the rest of the cow to rot. But no one complained; after all, it was either a juicy steak for supper or another K-ration meal of water, canned pork, crackers, and a bouillon cube.

In Luxembourg, Dad received his first wound of the war. His platoon had "dug in" on a hillside facing enemy lines and was providing direct fire support across a small river as infantry troops attempted a crossing.[22] No sooner had they started firing, when German artillery located them and began shelling their position. Dad recalls having a "funny feeling" that they were about to be hit and yelled to the rest of the crew to get out of the tank. He had just jumped off the hull of the tank when a German artillery shell hit the *We'll Make It*. Dad said it took him a while to "come to" because the explosion threw him several feet from the tank.

---

[22] In 1995 Dad sent me a newspaper clipping of a travel piece on Luxembourg accompanied by a photo of the picturesque hillside town of Chevaux. Dad said he recognized it right away as the town where his tank was hit while firing across the river valley at enemy positions.

It was then that he felt a burning sensation in his shoulder; a piece of shrapnel had passed through his jacket and shirt and lodged behind his left shoulder. Despite the injury, Dad said he felt lucky: two of his crew did not make it out of the tank. In a short visit to a field aid station,[23] medics removed the metal shrapnel and stitched him up. This would be the first of two wounds for which he would be awarded a Purple Heart Metal. Dad didn't think much of the honor, commenting that, "It doesn't take a whole lot of skill to get your ass shot off."

> **The Shirt Off His Back**
> I was a boy when Dad shared the story of his first wound. I remember asking him how much it hurt. Dad said that the wound wasn't too bad; what really hurt was when the medic took off his shirt. I remember asking, "Well, how bad could that be?" Dad pointed out that during battle, the inside of a tank would get very warm from the heat of the weapons, causing the crew to sweat. "Even when you weren't fighting, you'd still be in a humid crew compartment, wearing a wet uniform and damp coveralls." They would fight like this for days at a time, with no change of clothing and no showers. Eventually, the tank crews would get fungal infections that the GIs called the "creeping crud." When the medic took my shirt off, Dad said, "the skin on my back came off with it." Dad said it really hurt, but after treating his wound, "They just gave me a clean shirt and sent me right back to my unit."

---

[23] A forward, staffed medical treatment location provided by a battalion's service company. Aid stations could be an medical vehicle, a tent, or just as simple as a table in a protected area.

Rhineland

Following the Allies' successful defense of the Ardennes, most enemy forces were forced back beyond the German border. It was at this point that the German Army was ordered to regroup behind a system of fixed fortifications called the "West Wall" or what the Allies referred to as the "Siegfried Line." There, the Germans were told to remain and fight in defense of the Fatherland. Although the German commanders requested permission to withdraw further east, behind the natural barrier presented by the Rhine River, Hitler refused and ordered them to fight where they stood. The German combat divisions that remained west of the Rhine were cut to pieces and by late February, the Allies were close to the banks of the river. Hitler's orders would prove costly and result in losses

American troops passing through the Siegfried Line
Early 1945

to the German Army of over 400,000 casualties, including 280,000 prisoners.

> **Company Barber**
> Dad started cutting hair for members of his crew and got pretty good at it. Soon he had a larger cliental, that included many of the officers. Dad said the hair cutting job allowed him to get to know the commander of D Company, Captian Eugene Snyder, who he liked both as a person and a leader. Regular, friendly encounters with the commander and other officers of his company helped Dad to get noticed over many of the other tankers. Dad said, it also allowed him to "schmooze" a few extra rations and the occasional luxury (cigarettes, candy, or fruit) for his tank crew.

The Third US Army's advance into Germany was named "Operation Lumberjack" in what would later be dubbed by the press as Patton's "Race to the Rhine." As with the Battle of the Budge, D Company of the 749th Tank Battalion and Dad would be part of that effort.

After watching the movie *Patton* (1970), I asked Dad if he had ever met the General. Dad said, not personally but he did see him once as he passed by in a jeep. The General exchanged a little friendly banter with members of Dad's Company and shouted out words of encouragement. I asked Dad what he thought of him as a leader. Dad said that he, like most of the guys in his unit, thought very well of Patton. They believed if the "Old Man" asked them to do something it must be important. Dad said, "No soldier wants to die, but the thought of dying is tolerable if you believe your sacrifice serves a worthwhile purpose." The feeling among Dad's unit was that Patton wouldn't put them at risk unless they had a really good chance of "...kicking the enemy's butt."

It is not clear when Dad received his next promotion, but by the end of the Rhineland Campaign, he had become a staff sergeant or technician sergeant third grade (T/3). It is also at this point that Dad helped crew other tanks, including the smaller M5 Stuart and M24 Chaffee tanks.

T/3 Insignia

The Stuart tank was a light, four-man vehicle used to perform the traditional cavalry missions of scouting and screening.[24] The tank was lightly armored, equipped with a small 37 mm main gun, and three 30-caliber machine guns: one coaxial, one on the bow, and one on the turret. Dad did not like the Stuart tank, and although it was faster than the Sherman tank, Dad said that only meant "It just got you into trouble quicker."

Stuart light tank

Early in the war, the weaknesses of the Stuart became well evident and by the Rhineland Campaign, most light tank companies were being re-equipped with the larger Sherman tanks or with the Stuart's replacement, the new M24 Chaffee. Dad liked the four-man Chaffee. He

---

[24] Screening is when a smaller unit positions itself between the enemy and the larger main of friendly forces. The screening unit provides surveillance to the main body and skirmishes with enemy scouts.

said it was equipped with two eight-cylinder Cadillac engines, a four-speed transmission, and a torsion bar suspension, which made the M24 Chaffee faster, more reliable, and much more maneuverable than either the Sherman or the Stuart. The Chaffee also had a larger 75 mm main gun. Although it was still under-armored and vulnerable to most German anti-tank weapons, Dad said it was the best off-road armored vehicle of the war.

Chaffee light tank

The Third US Army now faced a largely disorganized enemy, but the Rhineland Campaign was no walk in the park. Besides being the first time the enemy was actually defending German soil, the advancing Allied armies were now confronted with the Siegfried Line.

The Siegfried Line was a 390-mile long barrier of moats, mine fields, tank traps, and bunkers. At key points behind the line's forward complex of moats, minefields, and tank traps, the German's located reinforced concrete bunkers, or "pill boxes" as GI's called them. These structures housed anti-tank or machine gun crews and their weapons. Several feet thick, with only a narrow slit for the gun barrel, these bunkers were impregnable to most Allied fire. Dad said, with 75 mm high-explosive or armor-piercing shells, it might take a Sherman or Chaffee tank all day to knock out a single bunker. One solution to this problem was the use of white phosphorous. Originally intended for creating smoke screens to hide friendly troop movements, American tank crews found the "smoke shell" useful as an incendiary against hardened targets. The phosphorous used in these shells, itself an oxidizer, did not require air to burn, could not be extinguished, and consumed almost anything as fuel. Besides producing a blinding flash, the phosphorous generated an enormous amount of dense, white smoke. Exploding a phosphorous shell in front of a bunker would, at a minimum, prevent the gun crew from seeing its target. This allowed Allied infantry sufficient cover to get behind the bunker, and using dynamite charges, blow open the bunker's rear steel door. Dad said that the use of phosphorous smoke and close coordination between tank crews and infantry resulted in many quick, successful attacks.

The Bunker

Dad's first use of phosphorous as an incendiary weapon was against the Siegfried Line. A machine gun bunker had halted infantry in an open field. Although partially undercover, the men were taking casualties and could neither advance nor retreat. Dad's tank was tasked with taking out the machine gun. To do this, they fired a phosphorous shell at the gun slit, where it burst, engulfing the structure in smoke, and spewing phosphorus through the slit. A moment later the rear steel door flung open and a German soldier stumbled out screaming. Chunks of burning phosphorous were buried in his flesh. Dad said he was mad with pain. But worst of all, his insignia showed that he was part of a Hitler Youth squad and was no older than about twelve. Horrified, the crew, dismounted the tank and tried to save the boy. "We held him down and cut out the phosphorous." Despite their efforts, the boy died of his burns. Dad said, it was bad enough seeing young men die a hard death, but the sight of a suffering child was unbearable. Afterward they told their lieutenant the army could court marshal them if it wanted, but they would never again obey an order to use phosphorous in such manner. For Dad, it was by far the worst experience of the war. He told me this story only once; it was obvious that some fifty years later, it was still difficult for him to share.

Dad's War

As fate would have it, the Rhineland Campaign would take Dad into the forested Eifel region, north of the Moselle River and by the "hometown" of his ancestors. Landkern, Germany is a small village located three miles north of the Moselle River town of Cochem in what is now the German State of Rhineland-Palatinate. Even today, Landkern has a population of fewer than one thousand residences and covers only about four square miles. Dad said he knew of the family's village from his grandmother, Regina Ungers, who had kept in touch with relatives before World War I.

Landkern, Germany
Fifty-five years later

Although unsure of the reception he would receive, Dad said it would have been interesting to meet a relative, but "…we passed by the town and didn't stop," and from what he could tell, the village appeared vacant and had sustained a fair amount of damage.

Wine Party

At one point, D Company was to cross a river to support an infantry unit that had already secured the opposite bank. The plan was for a platoon of combat engineers to erect a pontoon bridge before the appearance of Dad's tank company. Dad said they arrived at the appointed time to find the river, but no bridge and no engineers. A brief reconnoiter of a nearby village located the missing engineers. Discovering a wine cellar upon their arrival, the engineers had machine-gunned a number of large wine vats. The vats were huge and wine was pouring out through the bullet holes like so many garden hoses. The wine filled the cellar floor to a depth of several feet. The engineers were drunk to a man. Dad said it would have been funny but for the fact that a couple of the engineers had passed out on the floor and drowned in the raising pool of wine.

Dad's War

Crossing the Rhine

In March 1945, near the end of Operation Lumberjack, Patton's Third Army had reached the Rhine River with its left boundary, or "left flank," just north of Koblenz, Germany. The enemy was systematically destroying bridges over the Rhine in hopes of stopping the Allied advance. American, British, and Canadian armies all raced to the Rhine in hopes of being the first to capture a bridge intact. The First US Army under General Courtney H. Hodges got lucky and captured the Ludendorff Bridge at Remagen, Germany, on 7 March 1945. As advanced elements of Hodges' First Army approached the bridge, some of the demolition charges placed by the enemy failed to go off and the bridge, although badly damaged, remained standing. This stroke of good fortune would allow Hodges' troops to establish a bridgehead on the opposite bank of the Rhine and give the Allies their first foothold in the German heartland.

> **Death on the Homefront**
> Back in Mentor, Ohio, Dad's mother, Lena, died of a concussion after slipping on ice and hitting her head during the fall. Being at the front and in near-constant battle during January, Dad did not learn of her death until several weeks had passed. He said that he took the news very hard.

While the 749th HQ reports the battalion crossing the Rhine at Mainz, Germany, Dad remembered crossing at Remagen. Dad's remembrances don't coincide with the battalion's after action reports (AARs). However, Dad insists that D Company, or at least his platoon, crossed on the pontoon bridge constructed after the Ludendorff Bridge finally collapsed. This would have Dad crossing the Rhine sometime after 17 March and perhaps participating in the "breakout" from the Remagen bridgehead on 25 March 1945. Despite Dad's remembrances, it has to be said that most elements of Patton's Third Army, after reaching the Rhine in the vicinity of Remagen, did not cross there but turned south along the Rhine and either crossed at St. Goar or Mainz, Germany. It may be that Dad confused Remagen with either the St. Goar bridgehead or the Mainz location further south. Without backing away from his claim, Dad admitted to these possibilities, saying that he was never one hundred percent sure of the location of his platoon and added, "Hell, I was a nineteen-year-old sergeant. Most of the time, I only knew the location of the next hill we had to take!"[25]

On several occasions late in his service, Dad was the senior non-commissioned officer in his platoon, and had to take over when a tank commander was incapacitated. He must have been good at the leadership role, because by the time of the Rhine crossing, he had been offered a field promotion to first lieutenant. Dad said that being a commissioned officer had several attractive perks: better pay, opportunities for advancement, and, as Dad noted, "…the girls liked officers." However, the tank commander was the eyes and ears of the tank, requiring him to sit with his head outside the turret. This position exposed the commander to enemy fire, snipers, and shrapnel from overhead explosions. Dad said that he was ready to accept the offer when an older tanker pulled him aside and said, "Joe, you don't want to do this. You'll be safer remaining

---

[25] Dad's claim is possible for four reasons: 1) he remembers his company losing contact with the rest of the battalion; 2) he remembers fighting alongside the First US Army, elements of which crossed at Remagen; 3) the 749th's AARs are spotty with regard to D Company; and 4) Patton's left flank was only five miles from Remagen, but almost fifty miles from the Mainz.

a sergeant and staying a driver." In the end, Dad said he took the older soldier's advice. A replacement officer took over command and was fatally wounded within the week.

> **Summary Execution**
>
> Dad said he witnessed one summary execution during the war. He explained how tank platoons were supplied by their service company. A resupply truck, carrying fuel and ammunition, would be assigned to meet a platoon of tanks at a predetermined time and location. The importance of this meeting cannot be over stated: a missed encounter, or a delay in the arrival of supplies, could result in the loss of the tanks to enemy fire and countless casualties.
> Dad's platoon was supporting an infantry company when they ran low on fuel and ammunition and were pulled off the front line for resupply. When they arrived at the assigned location, the supply truck was nowhere to be found. By the time the vehicle arrived, the situation at the front had become serious due to the lack of armor support. The driver was found to be intoxicated and in possession of contraband that he had received in exchange for fuel. There was reason to believe the driver had traded other supplies for "favors" from a mademoiselle. The on-site commander was furious—one soldier had shirked his duty and put dozens of men at risk. He pulled out his service revolver and shot the driver in the head. Dad said no one protested; it was acknowledged without discussion— that the driver's behavior was beyond contempt and the punishment more than just.

Central Europe

Following the Rhine crossing, Patton's Third Army advanced into the German heartland and fanned out east into western Czechoslovakia, and southeast into Bavaria and northern Austria. Dad never identified any of the towns he passed through, nor did he mentioned exactly how far he advanced into Germany. Because of this, it is difficult to confirm whether he remained on the Third US Army's left flank or moved more to the main line of advance. He did say that they were heading for the Czech border and the capital, Prague.[26]

> **Expensive Entertainment**
>
> Once in Germany, tank platoons were ordered to destroy factories and heavy equipment that they encountered during their advance. It was feared that these assets could be used to prolong the war should they fall back into enemy hands. Dad told of his tank platoon coming upon a rail yard with several working locomotives. Rather than waste ammunition, they fired up the boilers on two locomotives, moved them to the same track, put them in gear, opened up the throttles, and watched the two locomotives collide at full speed! They did it again and again, until all the locomotives were destroyed. Dad said it was great fun.

With the end of the war in sight, Dad was having more contact with German civilians and captured soldiers. Having been raised in a

---

[26] At the end of the war, the battalion after AARs place D Company of the 749th Tank Battalion approximately 180 miles beyond the Rhine and near the town of Zietz in what is now the state of Saxony-Anhalt in April 1945.

German-speaking home, and not learning English until first grade, Dad was conversationally fluent—something he found very helpful.

> **Sprechen Sie Deutsch?**
> One night, Dad's tank had taken up a front line defensive position in a woods near a roadway. After several hours, they heard motorized vehicles approaching. "We couldn't see anything, but we were pretty sure it was a German patrol." Dad's tank crew didn't want to take on an enemy of unknown strength in the pitch dark, but nonetheless, they trained their guns on several dark shapes moving toward them. The patrol slowed down upon seeing their tank's silhouette among the trees. Someone from one of the enemy vehicles shouted out a question. Dad said he couldn't make it all out, but responded in his best German accent, "*Jawohl mein Herr!*" which is the equivalent of "Yes, Sir!" Nothing else was said and the patrol moved on. Dad added, "Either my response satisfied him, or they knew we were Americans, but like us, they just weren't in the mood for a fight."

Dad said he often spoke with prisoners and found the German soldiers' attitude to be "…pretty much like ours." Most were fighting, because they had been drafted or felt they needed to serve their country." However, Dad noted, the SS[27] were "…crazy bastards." The captured

---

[27] SS stands for Schutzstaffel, which is German for "protective shield." The SS was originally a peacetime paramilitary unit organized to served as Hitler's personal guard. During the war, the SS were converted into elite combat troops. Referred to as Waffen-SS, the number of Waffen-SS battalions would grow from three, at the start of the war; to thirty-eight, by the wars end. At the post-war Nuremberg trials the Waffen-SS was condemned for its involvement in war crimes. Waffen-SS troops were found responsible for the massacre of Jews, political prisoners, civilians, and the execution of American prisoners of war.

German soldiers were usually friendly, even if cautious; SS prisoners, on the other hand, were arrogant and menacing.

> **A Slippery Tank**
>
> According to Dad, the retreating enemy would place SS suicide squads in the path of their advance. Because the Allies were moving through villages that were still populated, when attacked, they couldn't return fire without the risk of injuring civilians. The SS took advantage of this and hid among the population. SS members would strap on large explosive charges and jump from rooftops onto Allied tanks, blowing up the tank and themselves at the same time. It occurred frequently enough that if an SS presence was suspected, tank crews would stop before entering a village, remove all the handholds from the outside of the tank, and cover the vehicle in axle grease. With their hatches closed, Dad said, "We would race through the town at full speed." On more than one occasion, "You'd hear someone praise Hitler, then through the tank's view ports, see a person pounce on the deck or turret, slip and slide, fall off the tank, and blow up in the road."

Casualty of War

I do not recall when, in April 1945, Dad received his second wound, but I do remember him describing the situation. He was in the driver's position of an M24 Chaffee as they were advancing down an open road. As they approached a tree line, the tank took a hit from what Dad believed must have been an 88 mm anti-tank gun. The force of the impact was massive. Dad said the armor-piercing shell hit the front of the tank, passed through the forward protective armor and the vehicle's transmission before entering the crew compartment between Dad and the bow machine gunner. It then deflected upward, grazing Dad's right knee. The shell then left the crew compartment through the ammunition storage bin before again penetrating the protective armor and exiting the tank. The

German 88 mm anti-tank gun

shell stopped the tank in its tracks and made it an easy target. The crew had to get out before the German anti-tank crew could reload and fire. Dad couldn't use his right leg and had to be pulled from the damaged vehicle. In their rush to get Dad out, his crew members further injured his already badly wounded knee. Dad said it looked and felt pretty bad, and he suspected that he'd be spending time in a hospital. Ultimately, this was the wound that would take Dad out of action and eventually send him back home.

Dad said that fate had again dealt him a good hand, because just before the hit on their tank, the crew had moved their 75 mm ammunition from a storage bin near him to another bin in the tank. Had they not done that, Dad said, the 88 mm shell would have struck the stored ammunition, exploded, and destroyed the entire tank—and everyone inside it.

Dad was driven by jeep to an Army aid station, where he received some basic treatment and morphine. The morphine relieved some of his pain, and he remembers drifting in and out of sleep. He was then loaded onto a medical evacuation plane that would airlift him to a field hospital somewhere in Belgium. Dad said, "As bad off as I was, the plane ride almost killed me." The aircraft was a single engine AeroMed L5 that was used to carry up to two wounded soldiers on stretchers.[28] The problem was that the little plane was not heated and the stretcher compartment was open to the air. Temperatures outside were well below freezing and Dad was sure he was going to freeze to death before they landed.

---

[28] As accessed on 1 June 2016 at https://www.med-dept.com/articles/ww2-air-evacuation.

AeroMed L5 single-engine aircraft

Dad had surgery in an American field hospital in Belgium before being transported by ambulance to Paris, where he would convalesce before being shipped back to the States. This last leg of Dad's war experience was unknown to me until late in his life. I took my family on a European vacation in the Summer of 2000. Afterward, we visited Mom and Dad at their home in Perry, Ohio, to share photos of the trip. When Dad saw a photo of Notre Dame, he remarked,"It looks just the way I remember it." Surprised, I asked him when he had ever been to Paris. At this point he shared the story of his journey after surgery and how he had recovered in a hospital directly across the street from the Notre Dame Cathedral. Back then, on nice days, Dad told us, the nurses would wheel the patients outside to get a little sunshine and fresh air. He spent several hours each day watching the people and the street traffic, and looking at the cathedral. Dad had been a Roman Catholic altar boy from a small rural town in Ohio, and so he was more than a little impressed, and remembered thinking, *"We sure don't build them like that back home."* The facility where he stayed was the Hospitel Hôtel-Dieu de Paris, the oldest medical facility in Paris, directly across from the cathedral, and it is still in use today.

Hospitel Hôtel-Dieu de Paris
(Notre Dame in the background)

Dad's War

Homecoming

Dad left France in early August and made an uneventful return crossing of the North Atlantic in a hospital ship. The ship arrived at the dockyards on Long Island on 14 August 1945—the day Japan surrendered. Still recovering and unable to walk, he was disembarked from the ship on a stretcher and was loaded into an ambulance, along with three other service men, for transfer to a hospital in New Jersey. There Dad would received therapy, and from there, he would be sent to Cleveland and then home.

> **Celebration**
> As luck would have it, the ambulance's route would take Dad through Times Square just as the victory over Japan was announced. Every office worker and shopkeeper in the city ran into the streets to celebrate. The traffic ground to a halt in the mass of humanity that had flooded Times Square! The crowd quickly realized that the ambulance he was in carried wounded GIs. Cheers went up as they forced open the doors of the ambulance. Complete strangers started shaking hands and hugging the men in the vehicle. Before long, bottles of beer and champagne were brought in and someone showed up with four steak dinners! Dad said it took hours to get out of Manhattan, but it was the best homecoming a guy could ask for.

Following his rehabilitation, Dad was put into another ambulance for the long drive from New Jersey to Ohio. The ambulance passengers included several wounded GIs—a few that were in serious condition—a doctor, and a nurse. Dad said he was able to walk fine, but the ambulance ride was mandatory transportation for a wounded soldier. Along the way, the vehicle stopped at several hospitals in Pennsylvania, dropping off the other returnees at facilities near their hometowns. By the time they reached Pittsburgh, only the driver, doctor, nurse, and Dad where still present. Dad told me that the doctor got off in Pittsburgh, which left the driver up front in the cab, and the nurse and Dad on board for the remaining trip to Cleveland. At this point, Dad smiled and said, "The nurse and I had a real good time in the back of that ambulance!" Pausing for a moment, Dad finished by adding, "...but don't tell your mother."

Although Dad's return home to America was great, his reception back in Mentor, Ohio, was not what you might think. His friends were happy to see him, but not all of his family. Dad's biggest disappointment was his maternal grandmother, Margret Wendlocker, a woman whom Dad said was authoritarian and generally disagreeable. She lived alone, estranged from her husband. Being a Roman Catholic, divorce was out of the question, so during his life Grandpa Wendlocker was seldom at his home in East Cleveland, where he and Margret owned a store. He preferred to live and work much of the year on his farm and orange grove in Punta Gorda, Florida. Dad remembered that when he went to visit his grandmother at her home in East Cleveland, she did not let him in the house, but met him on the front porch. Dad said, "I knew something was up." She looked him in the face and demanded to know, "*Haben Sie irgendwelche Deutschen töten?*" which in English is "Did you kill any Germans?" The tone of her voice was evidence of her bad mood. Dad told me, "I couldn't believe it. Her own grandson—a wounded veteran—and she was more concerned about the enemy!" Dad responded, as only

Dad would have, "YOU'RE GOD DAMN RIGHT I DID, GRANDMA!" Dad said she went to her grave never speaking to him again.

With his mother dead, the cool reception he received from some of his family, and the fact that his father, Henry, had to raise two of his younger siblings alone, Dad eased the situation by moving in with his good friend, Bill Edwards, a Navy veteran. On 6 October 1945, Dad was formally discharged from the army—a veteran of war at twenty years of age.

Bill Edwards and Dad
Fall 1945

Dad's War

Dad's decorations
Campaign ribbons
(three brass campaign stars are for:
Ardennes-Alsace, Rhineland, and Central Europe)
Expert medals   Battalion patch   Marksman medal
Purple Heart   World War II   Army of Occupation

Future Past

After the war, like thousands of other returning servicemen, Dad took advantage of the "GI Bill of Rights" and enrolled in college at Ohio University (OU) in Athens, Ohio. To supplement his government stipend, Dad won a wrestling scholarship that helped pay for classes and books. While at OU, Dad studied physical education with an eye to becoming a coach. He also joined the OU chapter of the Phi Kappa Tau fraternity—an organization that his grandson, Joseph Ungers, would also join some sixty years later, at Miami University of Ohio.

Between what he could make during the summers, the GI Bill, and his scholarship, Dad said, "I wasn't eating steak, but I was doing pretty well." Unfortunately, the modest financial stability Dad achieved was lost when OU dropped its wrestling program just before his senior year. Needing to replace the lost funds, Dad secured another wrestling scholarship at Ohio State University (OSU) and transferred to Columbus that fall. Unfortunately, most of his academic credits did not transfer and Dad only had enough to enter OSU as a sophomore. Dad "stuck it out" a couple of semesters, but said, "I just got tired of being poor." He also didn't like the idea of facing two more years of school before getting his degree. Dad decided to quit and find employment back in northeastern Ohio.

It was in Mentor that he would meet and marry Lilian G. Stampfel, help raise three children, and start three successful businesses: Middleton & Ungers Construction, a construction company Dad owned with a high school friend; Mentor Sand & Supply, a sand and gravel quarry; and Mentor Mini Storage, a commercial and retail storage business. He would also start and lead two local athletic organizations: Mentor Boosters, a club of business supporters of the local high school football team; and Bantam Football, a youth football league. Dad would also serve on the regional planning board and as a councilman on the Mentor City Council. Following a period of ill health, he retired in his fifties to a tract of rural acreage that he had owned since 1959. Located in Perry, Ohio, the property overlooks the Indian Point Metropolitan Park on the scenic Grand River. There he built a retirement home and "gentleman's farm" complete with a barn, fenced pastures, a working windmill, and a fishing pond. Spending summers in Perry and winters in Nokomis, Florida, Dad enjoyed his four grandchildren and pursued his two leisure time passions: fishing and restoring antique tractors. He experienced a long, happy, and active retirement before passing away on 30 June 2006 at the age of eighty.

Sergeant Ungers and a Sherman
Fifty-years later

Who Dad Was

Growing up during the Depression and serving in World War II had a profound effect on Dad. The 1930s showed him what difficulties people can face during hard times, and that employment was to be considered a luxury, not a burden. Although he would sympathize with the poor or unemployed, the war had taught him the virtues of drive, will, and self-reliance. As a result, he was intolerant of those who would not find a way to "pull themselves up by their own bootstraps." Like many of his generation, who can rightfully be described as hardworking, I think it is fair to say that Dad raised working to an art form. There were two things Dad could not tolerate: laziness and dishonesty. Even then, he might forgive "a little white lie," but being lazy was a sin beyond redemption.

To Dad, work was like an athletic competition: you go to sleep early, so you would be rested for work; you wakeup early, so you would have more daylight to work; you eat right, not for your health but so you would have the energy necessary to work. The employees of his construction company joked, "Joe worked us like the German Army was attacking and just over the next hill."

It wound be wrong to imply that Dad never had fun, or didn't enjoy a good time; it was just that work came first: always before play, often before family, and certainly before everything else. Dad also figured his approach to work was transferable to the next generation. All his children were expected to be "good workers," but as his firstborn and only son, I had the unenviable privilege of being Dad's earliest "recruit" to his school of philosophy. By junior high school, a certain "cadence" had entered my life. After school, I was expected to work. I often worked on Saturdays, either with him at a job site, in our home garden, or on acreage he had planted in corn or soybean. On Sundays, you got "time off," which usually meant helping Dad with a home project or going into his shop to hand him tools as he fixed a broken piece of heavy equipment. By high school, the level went up a notch, which meant construction jobs as a laborer during the summer and on holidays. I racked up countless after-school hours raising a barn, building a stone bridge, laying cobblestones, digging fence posts, bricking in sidewalks, and clearing land, usually by hand.

The Ditch

When I was home from college one summer, Dad bid on a construction job to dig a drainage ditch for a new strip mall. The construction drawings called for the ditch to be three feet deep, four feet wide, and three hundred feet long. Dad won the job based on the use of a backhoe and an operator, but instead gave it to me. Handing me a shovel, he said, "It's all yours. Should take you about two weeks." After a day or two working at what first appeared to be a thankless task, I noticed several older men from a nearby retirement community sitting on a bench watching me work. At lunch one day, I decided to introduce myself. I asked them if they sat out there often. One of them looked at me with a smile, saying, "Hell no, kid. We just came to watch you work. We haven't seen anyone dig a ditch like that since the Depression!" Hearing the remark, I have to admit, I was more than a little bit proud. Thanks Dad!

With Dad, as with his brothers, the Depression and time in the service taught them not only to work hard, but also "to do the job right" the first time. Like his brothers, Dad did not like sloppy work and wanted the job done just so. My cousin Bobby liked to make fun of our fathers' pickiness with a little quip he loved to tell. Bobby would comment, "You know, don't you, that there is the Ungers' way and the wrong way," then adding, with a grin, "and sometimes, the Ungers' way is the wrong way!"

It is sufficient to say, that Dad was not an easy-going parent. But he always "had your back" and he was there when you needed him. My mother—another child of the Depression—when seeing me frustrated or feeling sorry for myself, would trumpet my father's great virtue as only a Depression-era child could: "Your Dad may be a hard man to live with, but he loves you, and he is a good provider." Once, when I was a boy, listening to his stories, he summed up his personal philosophy, telling me, "Les, all life can expect of a man is that he be hardworking and honest."

Army Formations

(in descending order)

Army

100,000 to 150,000 troops, usually commanded by a lieutenant general (3-star) or general (4-star).

Corps

25,000 to 50,000 troops, usually commanded by a lieutenant general (3-star) and consisting of two or more divisions.

Division

10,000 to 20,000 troops, usually commanded by a major general (2-star) and consisting of several brigades or regiments of a total of eight or more battalions.

Battalion

400 to 1,000 troops, usually commanded by a lieutenant colonel, and consisting of six companies: a headquarters, service, one light tank company and three medium tank companies.

Company

100 to 250 troops, usually commanded by a captain and consisting of four units: a headquarters and three combat tank platoons.

Platoon

20 to 25 solders in five tanks and usually commanded by a lieutenant.

Bibliography

Action Against Enemy, After Action Report (AAR): *749th Tank Battalion.* (BiblioGov Project).

Access to Archival Databases (AAD). https//aad.archives.gov (accessed May 21, 2016).

Beevor, Anthony. *Ardennes 1944: The Battle of the Bulge/Hitler's Last Gamble.* (New York: Viking Press, 2015).

Hunnicutt, R. P. *Sherman - a History of the American Medium Tank.* 2cd Edition. (Novato, CA: Presidio Press, 1978).

Linduff, J. et al. "When Vice was King - a History of Northern Kentucky Gambling, *1920-1970."* Preserving Gaming History. http://www.preservinggaminghistory.com (accessed July 17, 2016).

Livingston, R. et al. *WWII Ballistics: Armor and Gunnery.* (Overmatch Press, 2001).

"M4 Sherman." Wikipedia. https//en.wikipedia.org/wiki/M4_Sherman (accessed May 10, 2016).

National Archives, *World War II Army Enlistment Records*, period ca. 1938–1946.

Patton, George S., Jr. *War As I Knew It (*The Great Commanders) (New York: Houghton Mifflin Company, 1994).

"P-47 Thunderbolt." Wikipedia. https://en.wikipedia.org/Republic_P-47_Thunderbolt.

"Perpetual Calendar." http://www.749thGenerations.org.

"Tiger II." Wikipedia. http://en.wikipedia.org/wiki/Tiger_II (accessed May 10, 2016).

Tillitt, M. *Barron's National Business and Financial Weekly*, April 24, 1944.

"WW2 Air Evacuation." WW2 US Medical Research Center. https://www.med-dept.com/article/ww2-air-evacuation (accessed June 1, 2016).

Yeide, Harry. *Steel Victory - the Heroic Story of America's Independent Tank Battalions at War in Europe.* (New York: Presidio Press 2003).

Zaloga, S. J. *US Tank and Tank Destroyer Battalions in the ETO 1944–45.* (Oxford: Osprey Publishing Ltd, 2005).